# Finlay and the Bogeyman

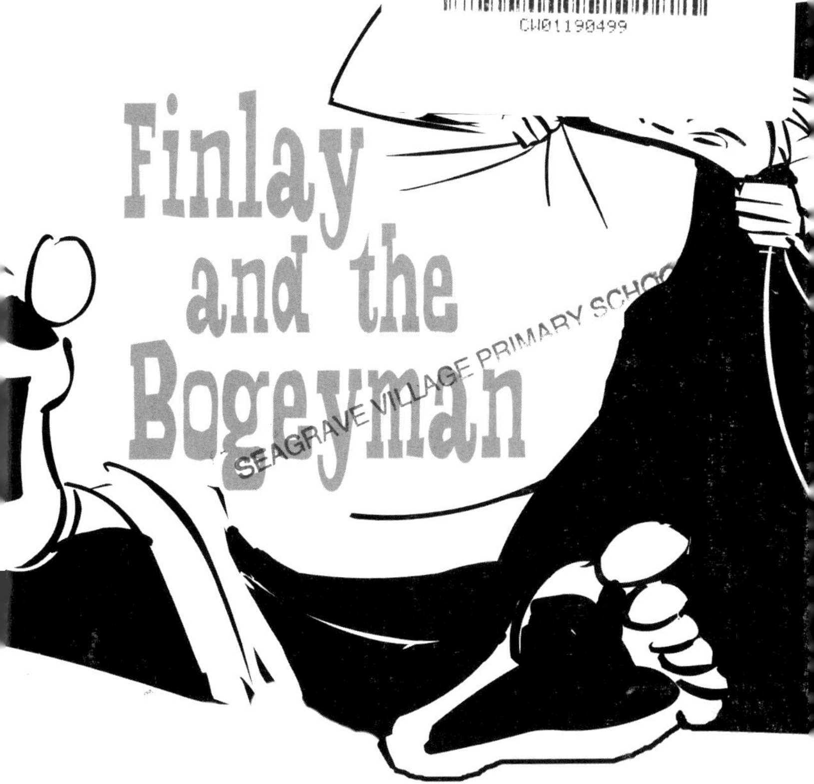



Steve Alton

Illustrated by Steve May

Ginn

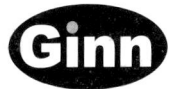

# Chapter 1

Finlay was a boy of very unpleasant habits. His sister, Freya, had one word for him: gross. Finlay spent most of his time in his room, slumped on his bed. There was a big TV screen on the wall, and every evening Finlay would lie there staring at the screen. By the flickering light of cartoons, his hand would creep up to his nose or ear and start to pick. Finlay's fingernails were bitten right down to the flesh, except for one. The nail on the smallest finger of his right hand was kept very long. He kept it like this for digging into awkward crevices.

He was using that fingernail now, poking away inside his ear. He pulled out a blob of earwax and, without taking his eyes from the screen, rolled it into a neat ball. He glanced down at the golden-brown lump, decided he was happy with its shape, and flicked it down the side of his bed. His hand wandered back up to his face. This time, the long fingernail disappeared into his nose. Finlay's nostrils were big and round, like two caves, from years of nose-picking.

The door banged open, and Finlay pulled his finger from his nose quickly. A small figure stood in the doorway, hands on hips. It was Freya.

"Finlay," she said, "get your finger out of your nose. It's time for dinner."

"Watchin' telly," grunted Finlay. "Bring it up on a tray for us."

"No way!" replied Freya. "I'm telling Mum. You are *so* in trouble!"

The door slammed and Finlay heard footsteps clatter downstairs. He sighed and turned back to the TV. His finger returned to his nose. He pulled out something rubbery and rolled it between his fingers. And then – flick. Off it went down the side of the bed.

Minutes later, the door flew open once more. This time it was Mum.

"Finlay," she shouted, "come and have your ... OH MY WORD!" Finlay's mum looked around the room, her mouth hanging open. "Finlay," she said, "this place is worse than ever! Look at it!"

Finlay looked. Dirty clothes were piled in heaps against the walls. Clean clothes hung out of drawers and mixed with the dirty clothes. Toys and games were scattered everywhere. Old pizza boxes and greasy plates lay on cupboards. A cup full of furry green mould stood beside the bed. There was a smell in the air of old trainers and sweaty socks.

Finlay looked back to his mum and shrugged.

"Right! That's it!" she shouted. "It's time there were some changes around here. Just you wait!" She slammed the door behind her and stamped off downstairs. Finlay heard angry voices. His parents were arguing. He sighed and slumped down on the bed.

Outside, beyond the curtains that never opened, the sun went down. Finlay's stomach began to rumble. Just as he was beginning to think he would have to get up, there was a soft knock at the door. "Yeah?" he called.

The door opened and Freya tiptoed in. She was carrying a plate.

"I brought you some dinner," she said. "It's cold, but it will have to do."

"Ta," grunted Finlay and grabbed it from her.

"Don't let Mum and Dad find out I brought you this. They'll go crazy. They had a huge row earlier, about you. Dad was all for locking you in the garden shed, but Mum calmed him down."

Finlay shrugged and carried on shovelling cold mashed potato into his mouth.

"You're an idiot," sighed Freya. "It wouldn't hurt just to tidy up once in a while, would it?"

Finlay shrugged again. "S'borin'," he mumbled around a mouthful of potato.

"Well," said Freya, getting up from the bed, "don't say I didn't warn you. See you in the morning."

Finlay burped as she closed the door quietly behind her.

He watched TV for another hour or so, but had trouble concentrating. He didn't like it when his parents argued. And deep down, part of him knew that he should make an effort to keep his room tidy. But it was so boring and most of the time he couldn't be bothered. Still, he couldn't help feeling guilty. Finally he gave up on the TV and, without bothering to wash or even to get undressed, he pulled the quilt over himself and settled down to sleep.

That night, shadows and the sound of angry voices filled Finlay's dreams. He felt a huge dark cloud gathering, as if a storm were coming. But it wasn't a rain cloud. It felt like black thoughts and unhappiness, piling up until he couldn't breathe. With a huge, shuddering sigh he groaned and turned over. The storm cloud drifted away and Finlay sank into a deeper, dreamless sleep.

# Chapter 2

The next day was a Saturday, so Finlay stayed in bed until eleven o'clock. When he could no longer force himself to sleep, he struggled upright and swung his legs over the edge of the bed. Looking down, he realised that there was no free space left on the floor for him to stand up in. So he flopped back onto the bed. Staring at the ceiling, his hand crept up to his ear and one finger disappeared inside. He stared into space, thinking about nothing, flicking the occasional pellet of wax down the side of the bed.

After a while, he decided his fingernails needed some attention. One by one, he carefully chewed off any bits of nail that stood free of the pink flesh. The long, white curls of nail he spat out, gathered up and dropped down the side of the bed. Next, he turned his attention to his feet. It was a while

since he had been in the bath, and his feet were rather scruffy.

As an experiment, he rubbed one finger between his first and second toes. As he rubbed, the dirt rolled up into long, brown sausage shapes. Pleased with himself, Finlay rubbed between all his toes, one after the other. The little sausages of dirt he flicked – as ever – down into the darkness at the side of his bed.

Around midday, the door flew open. Finlay yanked his finger from his nose and sat up. His mum stomped in. She was wearing an apron and bright-yellow rubber gloves. In one hand was a spray bottle of disinfectant. In the other was a feather duster.

"Right," she announced, "it's clean-up time!"

With that, she picked her way through the clutter on the floor and put the spray bottle down on top of a chest of drawers. Pausing, she looked around. It was difficult to know where to begin. Making her mind up, she went over to the wardrobe, kicking toys and clothes out of the way to make a path. Taking a deep breath, she grasped the two handles.

"Mum," began Finlay, "I wouldn't ..."

But it was too late. Finlay's mum pulled open the doors of the wardrobe and gasped. Like a tidal wave, a wall of dirty clothes hung above her for a moment and then, with a whump, crashed down on top of her. She stepped backwards, stumbled on a greasy plate and disappeared. Moments later, she burst up out of the mountain of clothes with a pair of Finlay's old underpants on her head. Like a swimmer coming up for air, her mouth opened and shut for a few moments. Finally, she gasped, "Finlay! You ... you ..." and then burst into tears.

Struggling up out of the heap, she ran for the door, smelly socks and old pants dropping from her as she went.

"Oh dear," thought Finlay. "I'm in serious trouble now."

Finlay followed his mum out of the room and paused on the landing. Downstairs, he could hear sobs and the sound of his dad's voice.

Finlay struggled to hear what he was saying.

"We should send for a doctor," his dad was saying.

"What do you mean, a doctor?" replied his mum, controlling her tears.

"You know, someone who deals with behaviour problems."

"Oh, no," sobbed his mum. "I'm not having him prodded and tested. He's not mad. He's just ... a bit lazy."

"A bit lazy! He's bone idle!" exclaimed his dad.

"Well, yes. But there must be another way, surely."

"Well," said his dad after a moment's thought, "there's one more thing we could try ..." His voice trailed away.

They had moved to the kitchen. Finlay hung over the banister, but try as he might, he could hear no more.

He marched back into his room and flung himself down on the bed. A feeling of panic came over him. This was getting serious. There was a real danger that he might have to do something. Even, maybe, tidy his room. But it was so unfair! He didn't bother anyone else. It was his room – they didn't have to come in. They should just leave him alone! He thumped the bed, sending a cloud of dust into the air. Coughing and spluttering, he turned on the TV and lay there brooding.

Towards the end of the afternoon there was a firm knock on his door. That was unusual – most people just burst in.

"Yeah?" he shouted.

The door opened. It was his dad. He looked uncomfortable. Shuffling in, he sat on the end of the bed.

"Son," he began, "the thing is, well, this has gone on long enough." He waved one hand at the mess around him. "It's upsetting your mother, and I can't have that. There have got to be some changes." He stood up and handed Finlay a piece of paper. "This is how things have got to be from now on."

Finlay took the piece of paper.

"You have a think about this, Son," his dad finished, and went to the door. With a last frown at the mess, he turned and closed the door softly behind him.

Finlay looked from the door to the piece of paper. He began to read. His mouth fell open.

"No!" he shouted. "No way!" And with that, he ripped up the paper and threw the pieces down the side of his bed.

# Chapter 3

Finlay sulked in his room until darkness fell. Once again, Freya had to bring him his dinner. Finlay barely spoke to her, even though none of it was her fault.

After she had gone, he lay in the darkness, staring at the TV. Its light flickered and danced on the walls. Finlay picked at a scab on his knee and stared at the screen until his eyelids began to droop. Then he rolled himself in the quilt and settled down to sleep.

In the still, black hours that follow midnight, Finlay's dreams turned dark once more. He felt as if he were lying on something unsafe – rotten wood that might give way beneath him. He didn't dare move in case the flimsy surface gave way. The air was thick with evil thoughts – too thick to breathe. Something waited beneath him, brooding, willing him to fall. He moaned in his sleep and turned over.

With a sudden feeling that he was falling, he woke up with a grunt.

Finlay sat up at once, his eyes wide open and his forehead damp with sweat. The bed felt solid beneath him. Of course, it had just been a dream. But the feeling of evil lingered. The sweat turned cold as Finlay sat in the darkness, staring out into the room. The faint orange glow of street lights came in through the heavy curtains. But rather than lighting up the room, it cast deep black shadows between the piles of clothes and rubbish. Finlay's ears strained to pick up any sound. A cooling radiator made a metallic tick and he jumped, then relaxed. Just the sounds of the old house settling into the night, he told himself.

Slowly, the silent darkness weighed down on him and, though he fought it as hard as he could, he began to nod. Lying back on the pillows he fell asleep once more.

Suddenly, he was awake again. He had no idea how much time had passed. Perhaps an hour, perhaps only a few minutes, but he knew instantly that something was in the room with him. He sat bolt upright, eyes wide with fright. Something moved, down at the foot of the bed. A small rustling sound and then – very clear – a sigh. Finlay opened his mouth and screamed.

The next morning, Finlay's mum made a big fuss of him. After his parents had come running and found him white and shaking in bed, he had spent the night in Freya's room. She had chatted to him about nothing much until he had fallen asleep. Now, he was tucking into an extra-big fried breakfast. As he ate, he could hear his mum talking to his dad in the next room.

"This is our fault," she was saying. "It's those stupid house rules. They've upset him."

"Rubbish," replied Dad. "It was just a bad dream."

"No, it's all the shouting and telling him off. He'll be wetting the bed next."

"All the more reason," replied his dad, "to take him to a doctor."

"Never mind the doctor," snapped Mum. "Just try being a bit nicer to him. Poor angel."

Finlay smiled and tucked into his fried bread and scrambled egg.

But the smile didn't last long. As the day went on, the thought of bedtime began to prey on his mind. For a change, he ate dinner with the rest of the family and sat with them in the living room.

Together, they watched TV and chatted, and Finlay was able to forget his fears. But as the evening wore on, his disturbed night began to take its toll, and he started to yawn.

After the fifth time, his dad said, "Looks like it's time for bed."

"No!" said Finlay sharply. "No, I'm fine. Really."

"Well," said Mum, "another half-hour, but no more. And do stop picking your nose, sweetie."

"Sorry, Mum," said Finlay, relieved, but his eye was now on the clock.

Finlay desperately stifled yawns and tried not to attract any attention to himself. But at last his dad glanced at the clock and said, "Right, young man – bed."

Finlay protested, but it was no use. His mum fussed around him and insisted on coming upstairs to tuck him in. He tried to drag it out, asking her stupid questions, pretending to have lost his pyjamas. But finally she kissed him on the forehead, turned out the light and closed the door.

Finlay sat very still in the darkness. At first,

he could see nothing. Then slowly his eyes grew used to the faint light from the curtains. He stared into the black pools of shadow, wishing he had tidied up. If the floor were bare, there would be fewer places where something could hide. His ears strained until he could hear the blood swish and surge in his head. His parents came upstairs and clattered around for a while. The toilet flushed and their bedroom door creaked shut. Silence settled.

It was very late when Finlay finally gave in to sleep. His head had been nodding for a while, but he had forced his eyes back open each time. Eventually, though, he could fight no more. He slumped back onto the pillow and let out a long, soft snore. Several hours later, in the dead of night, he began to moan and stir. He rolled back and forth, wrapped up in the quilt, as if wrestling with monsters. His bare feet, freed from the quilt, kicked around for a while, then grew still. Silence fell once more.

Then, in the darkness beneath the bed, something stirred. There were sighs and rustles. Suddenly, the bed sheet pulled tight as small hands grasped it. Something began to pull itself up, hauling itself hand over hand, up towards Finlay's feet.

# Chapter 4

Finlay screamed and clutched his foot. He fumbled for the bedside lamp and switched it on. Looking down, he saw that his big toe bore a circle of tiny red dots, like pinpricks. As he watched, they started to ooze blood.

He looked frantically around the room, but nothing was moving. He rubbed his toe and dragged the quilt back over him as the bedroom door flew open. Freya was first on the scene.

"What's up?" she asked breathlessly.

"There's something in here," Finlay replied. "It bit me. I think it's under the bed."

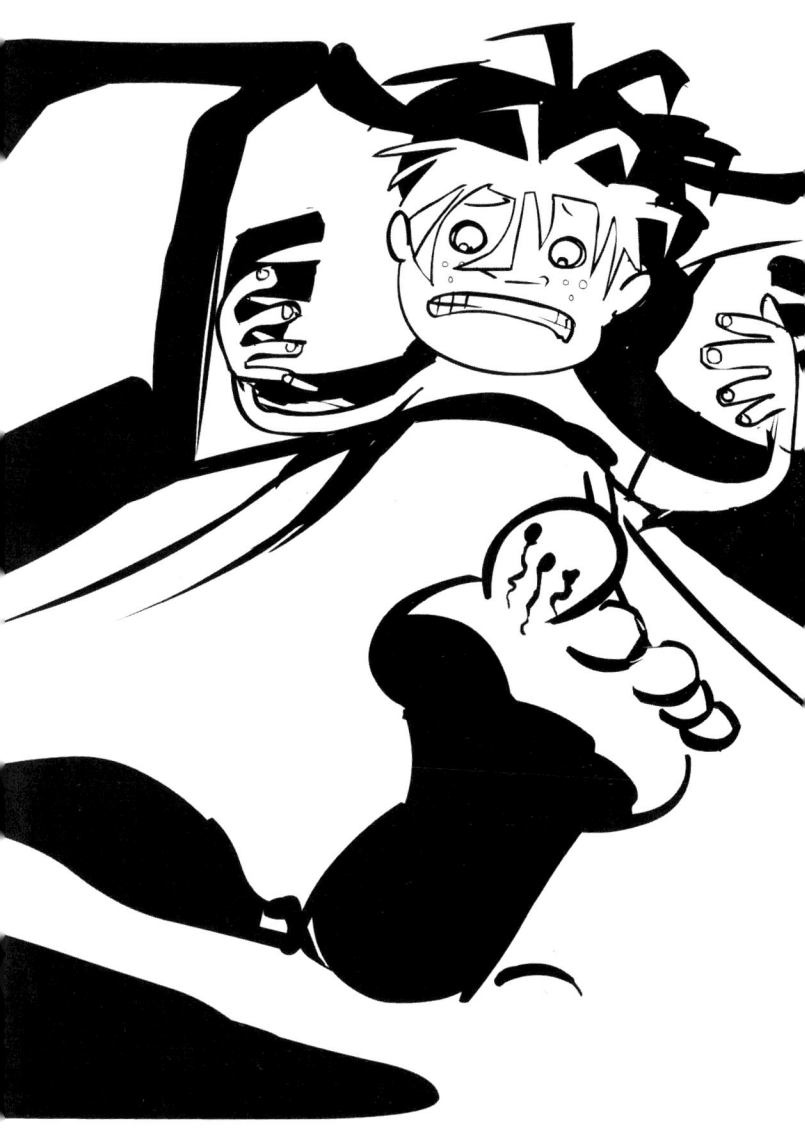

His mum and dad arrived at the doorway, looking bleary-eyed.

"What now?" demanded his dad.

"Finlay thinks there's a monster under his bed," answered Freya.

"Oh, for Heaven's sake!" exclaimed Dad. "How old are you?"

"Be nice!" snapped his mum. "Remember what we agreed."

"But monsters under the bed ..." began his dad.

"Come on, sweetie," continued Mum. "Sleep in your sister's room again."

Finlay was happy to obey.

Once again, Freya chatted to him to take his mind off his nightmares. But his thoughts kept returning to the dark presence beneath his bed.

"I'm not making it up, you know, Sis," he said, when Freya had fallen silent.

"Oh, come on," she sighed. "A monster

under the bed? That is so lame. It's just bad dreams."

"So how do you explain this?" he asked, and waved his foot at her.

"Urgh!" she said at first, then looked more closely. "Oh, wow! You've been bitten!"

"Exactly. So I didn't dream that part." Finlay looked smug.

"You know what probably did that, don't you?" asked Freya.

"Yes. A monster."

"No, you idiot. Rats!"

"No way!"

"Think about it. Your room's a tip. There are old bits of pizza and stuff all over the floor – you've got a rat."

"Well, that's it," sighed Finlay. "Mum and Dad are going to go spare."

"You don't have to tell them."

"I'm not leaving it there!"

"No, I mean, we could try to get rid of it."

"What, catch it?"

"Why not? We'll have an expedition tomorrow. See if we can trap it and throw it out. Okay?"

"Thanks, Sis."

"No problem. Now, get some sleep."

The next morning, Finlay and Freya met up in Finlay's room. Freya had borrowed a pair of thick leather gardening gloves from Dad, without him seeing. She also had a cardboard shoebox and a sturdy walking stick.

They sat side by side on the bed to discuss tactics. "Well," said Freya, looking around, "there are plenty of places where it could hide."

"It's under the bed," said Finlay.

"How can you be so sure?"

"I dunno. I just know. I've been having a bad feeling about it for a while now. I'm sure it's down there." He remembered the sense of lying on crumbling planks above something horrible. He shuddered.

"Okay," agreed Freya. "We'll start there. If we don't find anything, we'll work our way outwards."

She pulled on the gloves and handed the walking stick to Finlay. "Right, let's pull out the bed. Then I'll have a look down the side. Get ready to pass me the walking stick, okay?"

Finlay nodded. Together, they took hold of the edge of the bed and pulled. There was resistance for a moment, then it came free from the wall. A smell of damp drifted towards them.

Freya wrinkled her nose. "Okay, wish me luck," she said. "I'm going in."

And with that, she stretched out on the bed and hung her head over the edge. An unpleasant smell rose up to greet her, mould and dust and ... something else. Her stomach turned over and she swallowed hard.

It was dark and damp and very hard to see. Freya inched forward on the bed and pushed her head further down between the mattress and the wall. Her muffled voice came back to Finlay. "It's foul down here! You really are a pig!" She dragged herself a little further forward and swung one hand down into the darkness. Groping around, she felt something solid and grasped it in her gloved hand. Bringing it up out of the gloom towards

her face, she saw it was a plastic soldier with its head chewed off. She threw it up onto the bed behind her.

"That's where it went!" exclaimed Finlay, picking it up. "I've been looking for that."

Freya groped around a little more. It was no use – the leather gloves were too thick. She couldn't feel very much with them on. Reluctantly, she pulled the glove off her right hand and threw that back onto the bed.

Pulling a face, she put her bare hand back down into the darkness and stretched out her fingers. The carpet was sticky and damp, and there were crumbs or something scattered thickly across it. "The things I do for you," she muttered. There was nothing directly beneath her, so she moved her groping hand out sideways, following the skirting board.

"Hold my feet," she said to Finlay. "I need to reach a bit further."

Finlay grasped her ankles and she wormed her way forward until she was hanging right down the side of the bed with the blood rushing to her head. Her fingers crept along the carpet until she was at full stretch. Then, when she could reach no further, her fingertips brushed something, and she screamed.

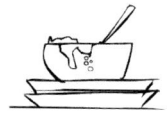

# Chapter 5

Finlay yanked Freya by the ankles, dragging her backwards across the bed. "What is it?" he demanded.

"I think," replied Freya, "it used to be a doughnut. But it's gone all green and furry. And I put my bare hand on it! You really are gross."

"Sorry." Finlay looked embarrassed. "So, no sign of a rat, then?"

"Nope. Though there'd be plenty for it to eat." Freya scowled. "Come on – let's move some of this other stuff."

For the rest of the morning, they dragged piles of clothes and boxes of computer games around the room. Each time they moved a new pile, they tensed, waiting for movement. But nothing happened. Eventually, they lost interest.

"I don't think we're going to find anything,

Fin," sighed Freya. "Face it – there's nothing here."

Finlay looked doubtful. "Well," he said, "I suppose not. But that doesn't explain the bite on my toe."

"Perhaps it was bugs. You know – some kind of mosquito."

"Bloomin' big mosquito!" exclaimed Finlay. "Nearly took me toe off!"

"Don't be such a baby. Anyway, I'm off. See you at lunch."

"Yeah, see you. And thanks, Sis!"

Freya returned to her own room. She had something on her mind, something she had found down the side of Finlay's bed.

Closing the door behind her, she sat down at her desk. From her pocket, she pulled a handful of strips of paper. They had been scattered on the floor by the skirting board, where Finlay had dropped or thrown them. Freya wasn't sure why she had picked them up. At first, she had planned to hand them back to Finlay. But then curiosity had stopped her. What was on the piece of paper, and why had Finlay ripped it up? In case it turned out to be a love letter from a girl at school – unlikely, she knew – she had stuffed the pieces in her pocket. Now, she spread them out on the desk before her.

To her surprise, she recognised her dad's handwriting. The strips were crumpled, so she smoothed them down and began to arrange them. She had always been good at jigsaw puzzles, so she soon found two pieces that went together, and then a third. After a few minutes, she had all the pieces matched up. But there was a gap – a piece was missing. It had been very dark down the side of the bed, but she was pretty sure she had picked up all the bits of paper down there. Strange. She sat, lost in thought, staring at the pieces of paper in front of her.

That evening, Finlay seemed a little happier. Though he was still not convinced that rats were to blame for his disturbed nights and the bite on his toe, at least they had failed to find anything in his room. Once more, he spent the evening with the rest of the family downstairs but, when bedtime came, he was less reluctant to go to bed.

Once again, his mum tucked him in and kissed him goodnight. The light went out and the door closed. Finlay sighed and stared into the darkness for a while. Freya had tried to tidy up a little as they had moved things around, and there were fewer big piles of toys and clothes in the room now. The pale orange light from the window even spilled across some patches of bare carpet. Even so, Finlay was aware of the darkness that must still lurk beneath his bed. But the morning's activity had left him tired, and the horrors of the night seemed less real. He was soon asleep.

Once more, in the stillest part of the night, Finlay began to stir. And once more, at the foot of the bed, small hands grasped the sheet and began to pull. Slowly, the creature dragged itself up onto the bed. Grabbing handfuls of the quilt, it pulled its misshapen body across the rumpled landscape, heading for Finlay.

With an effort, it reached the long ridge that marked his sleeping body. Somewhere around his knees, it pulled itself up onto his legs.

Finlay moaned. The feeling of pressure on his legs filtered down into his dreams. He swam up out of sleep, like a swimmer coming up from deep water. The creature tensed, hunching its body, bracing its legs. As Finlay opened his eyes, it sprang at his face.

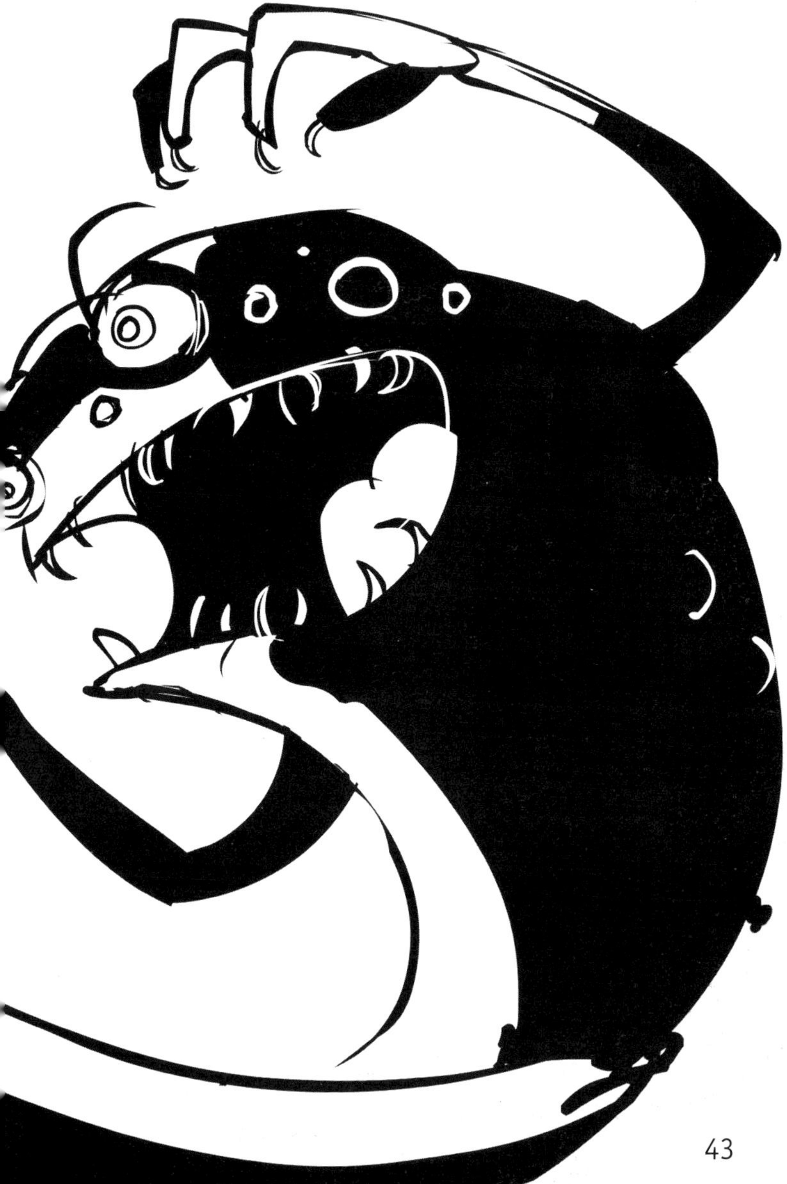

# Chapter 6

Finlay threw his arms across his face, and the creature bounced off, landing in his lap. "Get off me!" bellowed Finlay.

The creature scrabbled for a handhold in the folds of the quilt. In the dim orange light, it was hard to make out the details. Finlay had a glimpse of a gnarled, warty face and a mouthful of tiny, curved white teeth, before the creature sprang again.

Once more, Finlay threw up his arms and fended the creature off. It felt sticky, almost rubbery, against his bare skin. And it had a smell that made Finlay want to gag. It tumbled to a halt further down the bed and struggled to right itself. Scrambling back to its feet, it glared at Finlay and bared its teeth. To Finlay's surprise, it spoke. "Golem has its orders!" it croaked in a tiny, rasping voice. "Golem has its orders!"

As it crouched to spring once more, Finlay kicked out with his legs beneath the quilt, sending the creature flying. "Go away!" he shouted.

The creature hit the bottom of the bed and rolled, coming to a halt right on the edge. Hanging for a moment from the bed sheet, it cocked its head on one side. The door flew open and Dad burst in. By the time he had flicked on the light switch, though, the creature had released its grip on the sheet and dropped down out of sight.

"It's there!" shouted Finlay. "A monster! Right there! Did you see it?" Finlay was bouncing up and down on the bed, pointing frantically.

"Finlay, calm down!" shouted his dad. "It's just a bad dream!"

"It's not! It's real! It was right there!"

Finlay's mum came in, wrapping a cardigan around her shoulders. She sat on the foot of the bed. "There, there, sweetie," she said. "I know it seems real, but it was only a dream." Dad stood in the middle of the room, shaking his head. "That's it," he muttered. "That's the last straw."

Finlay was sobbing now, partly with relief that the creature had gone, partly with frustration that no one would believe him. Mum put her arm around him. "Come on, precious," she said, "into your sister's room again."

Finlay allowed himself to be led, shaking, to Freya's room.

" ... and it jumped straight at me! Right at my face!" Finlay was wrapped in a blanket on the floor by Freya's bed. He stared into space, eyes wide, as he told his sister what had happened.

"And what did it look like?" asked Freya. She was lying on the bed facing him, propped up on her elbows.

"Well, it was difficult to see, because it was

dark. But it looked sort of brown, or green. And lumpy. Like a kid's model in clay. Not a very good model. And it was a bit furry in places. And it had a mouth full of teeth. Thin, curved teeth." Finlay shuddered at the memory.

"Anything else?" Freya asked. She was starting to believe her brother. He was too scared to be making it up.

"It ... it said something."

"It spoke?" Freya looked doubtful. "What did it say?"

"Well, it sounded like 'Golem has its orders.' Something like that."

"Are you sure? Try to remember – this is important."

"Pretty sure, yes. 'Golem'. That's what it said."

"Try to get some sleep. Tomorrow, I'm going to try to find out what this thing is, once and for all."

The next day, after school, Freya closed the door of her bedroom and switched on her computer. Logging on to the Internet, she opened up her browser and typed in 'Golem'.

Then she hit the 'Search' button. She sat back as the results popped up on the screen.

Half an hour later, she rubbed her eyes and sighed. There was plenty of information out there about Golem, and she had read through an awful lot of it. From a drawer in her desk, she took out the pieces of paper she had found down the side of Finlay's bed. Once more, she spread them out in front of her. If only she could work out what the missing strip of paper had said. That was the key to the whole business.

The first missing word was obviously 'Finlay'. The second one could be 'to', or possibly 'must'. Probably 'must', judging by the size of the space it had to fill. But the last word ...

Gurgle
golem
FOR - LIST OF CH ORES
ALL CLOTHES BE FOLDED
NO TV UNTIL HE TI S HIS ROOM
IN BED BY 9.30
UP BY 7.30
NO FOOD IN THE BEDROOM

She sat and stared at the jigsaw puzzle before her. Well, whatever the missing word was, she had a pretty good idea now what they needed to do.

She turned off her computer and went downstairs. Finlay was in the living room, watching TV as ever. Freya flopped down on the sofa beside him. "Fin," she said, "we have a job to do."

Finlay groaned. "Not more tidying up?"

"Sort of," Freya smiled. "This monster of yours ..."

"What about it?" Finlay looked more interested.

"I know what it is now. And I think I know how to get rid of it." She allowed herself to look smug.

Finlay sat up and turned to her, eyes wide. "Really?"

"Yup. And tonight, big brother, you and I are going monster-hunting!"

# Chapter 7

Later that afternoon, Finlay wandered through to the kitchen in search of a snack. His dad was on the telephone. In the doorway, Finlay paused – he had heard his own name mentioned. Staying out of sight, he strained to listen.

"That's right," his dad was saying, "disturbed sleep, nightmares, and now he's convinced there's a monster under the bed." There was a pause. "Yes, he's eleven. That's right." Another pause. "No, not really. Well, we've had a few arguments about his room. Tidying up, that kind of thing. But no, otherwise he's pretty happy." Pause. "Great – half-past four tomorrow. Thanks, Doctor. See you then." His dad put the phone down.

Finlay turned and ran upstairs. "Hey, Sis!" he shouted, bursting into Freya's room.

"Can't you knock?" she snapped.

"This is important! Dad's just been on the phone to the doctor."

"So?" Freya looked puzzled. "Is somebody ill?"

"No, you idiot, not the doctor – the doctor!"

"What do you mean?"

"The shrink! They think I'm mad. The doctor's coming tomorrow. Probably going to take me away!"

"Well," said Freya, shutting her book, "we'd better make sure we get this sorted out tonight then. Remember what we agreed?"

Finlay nodded.

"Good. I'll see you later."

That night, after everyone had gone to bed, Freya let herself into Finlay's room and closed the door behind her. Saying nothing to her brother, who was watching her from his bed, she crossed the room and settled into a comfortable chair. Taking a deep breath, she prepared herself for a wait.

The long, slow hours of the night passed. Freya fought off sleep and the urge to move, stretch her legs, or yawn. Finlay was less quiet – from time to time she heard him stir, turning over and sighing. She was fairly sure, though, that he was still awake as they had agreed. Then, at some point in the early hours of the morning, she heard a snore. Freya's eyes went wide. The idiot! He'd fallen asleep after all. She looked around for something to throw, but there was nothing to hand. She sat in frustration, praying that he would wake up. And then, perhaps half an hour later, she saw it.

In the dim orange light, she caught a glimpse of movement at the foot of the bed. She froze. There was no way she could warn her brother without spoiling the plan. She had to force herself to watch as a dark shape pulled itself free of the shadows and clambered onto the bed. Slowly, it made its way up the quilt, towards Finlay's chest. Finlay sighed in his sleep and then rolled his head to one side.

The creature paused. It adjusted its feet, preparing to spring. Freya leaned forward silently in her chair, willing Finlay to wake up. The creature opened its mouth and the pale light glinted on rows of tiny teeth. It shifted its feet one last time, making sure of its grip, and launched itself at Finlay's throat.

Suddenly, Finlay shot upright in the bed, bringing the quilt up with him. Instead of landing on Finlay, the creature found itself wrapped in cloth. "Now, Sis!" said Finlay. After a moment of surprise, Freya snapped on the huge torch she had taken from Dad's shed. The powerful beam stabbed out, lighting up the bundle on the bed. Screwing her eyes up against the glare, she rushed to her brother's aid. The creature squirmed and writhed in the folds of quilt as Finlay struggled to hold it. Freya switched on the bedside lamp and crashed down on the bed next to him.

Together, they tried to pin the creature

down, but it was too strong. One arm broke free, and then another. With a wrench, the creature was loose. It scuttled back, towards the foot of the bed, where it paused. It seemed to be debating whether to attack again or retreat back under the bed. Freya swung the torch around and fixed it in the beam.

Her stomach lurched as she realised that her guess had been right. As Finlay had said, it looked like a child's model in clay. Only it was made of something far less pleasant than clay. Everything that Finlay had dropped down the side of his bed over the years – earwax, scabs, belly-button fluff and worse – had somehow moulded together to form this creature. The torchlight glistened on its damp, lumpy skin. Freya saw that each of its teeth and claws was, in fact, one of Finlay's fingernails, thin and white and curved. She felt sick.

The creature made up its mind. Without warning, it sprang again.

"Grab it, Fin!" Freya hissed.

Startled, Finlay just had time to throw up his hands as the thing flew through the air towards him. He caught it around the waist, but was thrown back against the headboard by the force. It writhed and wriggled in his grasp, its teeth snapping only inches from his face. The smell of its breath was foul.

"Hang on – I'm coming!" Freya scrambled down the bed and seized hold of the creature, grabbing it around the legs. "Right," she said, "do what I told you!"

Finlay let go with one hand, flinching as the thing lurched closer to his face for a moment. But Freya had a firm grip.

Screwing up his face, Finlay plunged his fingers into the creature's gaping mouth. The tiny teeth closed on his flesh and he winced. Fighting his feeling of horror, he pressed deep until he found what he was looking for. Then, in triumph, he pulled out a piece of paper.

Instantly, the creature fell apart in their hands. A shower of nameless crumbs and bits of fluff rained down on the bed as Freya fell over backwards and Finlay slumped back against the headboard. It was over.

# Chapter 8

"So, this thing ..." Finlay asked Freya in the darkness of her bedroom.

"Golem," corrected Freya.

"Right, this golem," continued Finlay, "you reckon it just formed somehow, under the bed?"

"Don't ask me how, but yes. Out of all the horrible bits of yourself you dropped down there over the years."

Finlay looked thoughtful, and a little embarrassed.

"There's an old legend about the golem," Freya continued. "The first one was made by a Rabbi – that's a Jewish priest – in Germany. He made his out of clay, though, and brought it to life by magic. And he used to give it instructions by writing them on bits of paper and putting them in its mouth. I read about it on the Internet. It used to do chores, until it got out of control."

"So when I dropped that piece of paper down there, that gave this thing an instruction?"

"Yes – 'Finlay must die'. I couldn't work out what the missing word was, but I was sure that must be where the piece of paper had gone."

Finlay shuddered. "Good job you were right." He looked down at his hand, which was covered in tiny pinpricks. "I still don't understand how the golem came to be in the first place, though."

"Neither do I," said Freya, "but you can be sure of one thing."

"What's that?"

"You brought it on yourself."

Finlay was silent, staring into the darkness. "Hey, Sis?" he said at last.

"Yes?"

"Do you suppose that's where the name 'bogeyman' comes from?"

"Don't be gross!" Freya threw a spare pillow at him. "And go to sleep."

"Goodnight, Sis." Finlay smiled in the darkness.

"Goodnight."

The next morning, Finlay was missing from breakfast, and Freya was sent to find him. She made her way upstairs and headed for her brother's bedroom. Pausing in the doorway, she looked in.

The room was transformed. All the rubbish was bagged up in black bin liners and was waiting to be thrown away. The mountains of clothes were gone and all the toys and video games were in boxes neatly lined against the wall. The bed had been dragged into the centre of the room, and at first there was no sign of Finlay.

Freya took a step through the doorway and spotted him. He was on his hands and knees on the floor where his bed used to stand. He was wearing a pair of bright-pink rubber gloves and an apron, and he was busily scrubbing away at the skirting board. A bottle of bleach and a bowl of water stood beside him.

Freya edged back out of the room. Smiling to herself, she turned and headed back downstairs, to tell her parents that Finlay was all right.